NOT-SO-

# GET SMELLY WITH SCIENCE!

PROJECTS WITH ODOURS, SCENTS AND MORE

by Elsie Olson

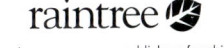

raintree
a Capstone company — publishers for children

Raintree is an imprint of Capstone Global Library Limited, a company incorporated in England and Wales having its registered office at 264 Banbury Road, Oxford, OX2 7DY – Registered company number: 6695582

www.raintree.co.uk
myorders@raintree.co.uk

Hardback edition text © Capstone Global Library Limited 2023
Paperback edition text © Capstone Global Library Limited 2024

The moral rights of the proprietor have been asserted. All rights reserved. No part of this publication may be reproduced in any form or by any means (including photocopying or storing it in any medium by electronic means and whether or not transiently or incidentally to some other use of this publication) without the written permission of the copyright owner, except in accordance with the provisions of the Copyright, Designs and Patents Act 1988 or under the terms of a licence issued by the Copyright Licensing Agency, 5th Floor, Shackleton House, 4 Battle Bridge Lane, London, SE1 2HX (www.cla.co.uk). Applications for the copyright owner's written permission should be addressed to the publisher.

**British Library Cataloguing in Publication Data**
A full catalogue record for this book is available from the British Library.

ISBN 978 1 3982 4558 7 (hardback)
ISBN 978 1 3982 4557 0 (paperback)

**Editorial Credits**
Editor: Jessica Rusick
Designer: Aruna Rangarajan
Originated by Capstone Global Library Ltd

**Image Credits**
iStockphoto: malerapaso (herbs), Front Cover, 4, assalve (spices), 4, 13, colevineyard, 4 (soap), fcafotodigital (essential oils), 4, 20, Joe_Potato (vanilla extract), 4, 16, marilyna (wildflowers), 4, 22, Photograpther, 4 (crayons), Christopher Ames (essential oil and rosemary), 6, 18, lucop, 31 (gardenia in vase); Shutterstock: ONYXprj (background), Front Cover, Back Cover, Lunik MX (bubbles), Back Cover, 6, 7, Elizabeth A.Cummings (food colouring), 4, 26, Mega Pixel (glue), 4, 16, Natakorn Ruangrit, 4 (scissors), thoughtsofjoyce, 6 (glycerin), Sergei Bogachov, 8 (glue gun), SweetLemons, 8 (googly eyes), virtu studio, 8 (eggs), Kalfa, 9 (rotten fruit), conzorb (microwave), 10, 25, ChristianChan, 12 (question marks), dezign56, 12 (glue stick), Regine Poirier, 12 (dryer sheets), pikepicture, 14 (grater), Sarah2, 15 (tea bag), Agave Studio, 18 (white flowers), MakroBetz, 18 (brass brads), Vladimirkarp, 18 (pine branch), Simone Andress, 19 (fir needles), Freer, 20 (matchbox), Free Life Design, 23 (orange peel), koosen, 24 (rice in bowl), phil_berry, 24 (socks), Denphumi, 26 (paintbrushes), Lukas Gojda, 26 (painted background), Sheila Fitzgerald, 26 (almond extract), Thesamphotography, 26 (lemon), Mega Pixel, 27 (rainbow picture), Africa Studio (chamomile flowers), 30, 31, cameilia, 30 (gardenias), Daniel Prudek (bee), 30, 31, ehtesham, 30 (bee on flower), Butterfly Hunter, 31 (butterfly)

**Design Elements**
Shutterstock: MicroOne (gauges), WhiteBarbie (calendar date)
All project photos shot by Mighty Media, Inc.

Every effort has been made to contact copyright holders of material reproduced in this book. Any omissions will be rectified in subsequent printings if notice is given to the publisher.

All the internet addresses (URLs) given in this book were valid at the time of going to press. However, due to the dynamic nature of the internet, some addresses may have changed, or sites may have changed or ceased to exist since publication. While the author and publisher regret any inconvenience this may cause readers, no responsibility for any such changes can be accepted by either the author or the publisher.

Printed and bound in India

# CONTENTS

Make a stink! .................... 4
Scented bubbles .................. 6
Monster stink bomb ............... 8
Smelly soap explosion ........... 10
Memory match game ............... 12
DIY tea soap .................... 14
Birthday batter slime ........... 16
Scent scrapbook ................. 18
Calming crayon candle ........... 20
Season in a jar ................. 22
Not-so-stinky sock .............. 24
Scratch & sniff paint ........... 26
Smelly trainer swab ............. 28
Flower power .................... 30
Find out more ................... 32

# MAKE A STINK!

What happens when scents are sweet or experiments reek? It turns out that super smelly science projects also happen to be fantastically fun. So grab your gloves, put on your lab coat and breathe in deep.

**THINGS ARE ABOUT TO GET SMELLY!**

## GENERAL SUPPLIES & TOOLS

- bar of soap
- crayons 
- essential oils 
- flowers 
- food colouring 
- herbs 
- PVA glue 
- scissors 
- spices 
- vanilla extract

# TIPS & TRICKS

**FOLLOW THESE SIMPLE TIPS TO STAY SAFE AND HAVE FUN!**

- **Read all the steps** and gather all your supplies before starting a project.

- **Beware of working with essential oils.** Don't swallow oils, put them directly on your skin or use them around pets. Wear gloves when working with essential oils. And remember that a few drops go a long way!

- **Wash your hands** after handling slime.

- **Ask an adult** to help when using hot or sharp tools.

# SCIENCE TERMS TO KNOW

**DENSE:** having a high mass compared to volume

**MOLECULE:** two or more atoms bonded together

**NEURON:** a nerve cell that communicates with other cells in the nervous system using electrical signals

**OLFACTORY:** relating to the sense of smell

**POLLINATOR:** something, usually an insect, that pollinates flowers. Pollination is the process of carrying pollen from the male part of a flower to the female part.

# SCENTED BUBBLES

Make colourful bubbles that **smell sweet** as they pop!

**EXPERIMENT! MAKE DIFFERENT WAND SHAPES. DO SOME WORK BETTER THAN OTHERS?**

## WHAT YOU NEED

- jug
- ¼ litre (1 cup) unscented washing-up liquid
- 22 millilitres (1½ tbsp) glycerine
- 1.4 litres (6 cups) water
- mixing spoon
- 3 jars with lids
- food colouring
- essential oils
- pipe cleaners

## WHAT YOU DO

### STEP 1
In the jug, mix together washing-up liquid, glycerine and water.

### STEP 2
Divide the mixture between the three jars. Add different food colouring and essential oils to each jar.

### STEP 3
Bend a pipe cleaner in half. Twist the ends together, making a loop about 6 centimetres from the top. This is your bubble wand.

### STEP 4
Pour a bit of scented liquid into each jar lid. Dip the wand into the liquid and blow a bubble. Try each scent. Which bubbles smell the strongest?

## WHAT YOU GET

**Molecule magic!** From freshly baked bread to stinky rubbish, every object you smell gives off odour molecules. These molecules are usually lightweight enough to travel through the air. When you blow a bubble, it releases essential oil molecules, dispersing the scent! **That's science!**

# MONSTER STINK BOMB

Turn ordinary kitchen items into a DIY stink bomb with a **stench so strong** it could clear a room!

## WHAT YOU NEED

- container with lid
- raw egg
- 15 millilitres (1 tablespoon) milk
- 15 ml (1 tbsp) vinegar
- art supplies, such as a hot glue gun, tin foil, pipe cleaners & more

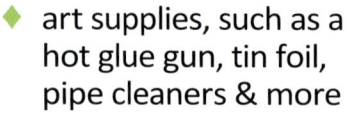

## WHAT YOU DO

### STEP 1
Break the egg and drop it into the container.

### STEP 2
Add the milk and vinegar. Put the lid on the container and give it a shake to mix up the ingredients.

### STEP 3
If you'd like, decorate the container to look like a monster or other scary creature. Then put the container in a safe place for five to seven days. The longer it sits, the smellier it gets!

### STEP 4
Remove the lid from your container and leave it where someone can smell it but not see it. Pee-ew!

## WHAT YOU GET

**Stinky for safety.** Bacteria grow on food as it spoils. Both the bacteria and the rotting food release chemicals that smell bad. Bad smells like rotten eggs, spoiled milk or mouldy fruit are a signal to your brain. They tell you something is unsafe and could make you sick. **That's science!**

# SMELLY SOAP EXPLOSION

What happens when you put soap in the microwave? Try this **soap-scented experiment** to find out!

SMELL-O-METER 5

## WHAT YOU NEED

- Ivory brand bar soap
- another brand of bar soap
- tub or sink filled with water
- plate
- sharp knife & cutting board
- microwave

10

## WHAT YOU DO

### STEP 1
Place both soaps in the water. Note whether they float or sink.

### STEP 2
Cut a 2.5-cm (1-inch) piece of each type of soap and put on a plate.

### STEP 3
Microwave the soaps for 1 minute. What happens? How did the floating soap react differently from the non-floating soap?

## WHAT YOU GET

**Expanding soap.** Air is whipped into Ivory soap as it is manufactured. This makes it less dense than water, so it floats. The tiny air pockets contain water molecules. When heated, the water expands in the air pockets. This makes the soap puff. **That's science!**

# MEMORY MATCH GAME

How much does your nose know? Find out how good your **scent memory** is with this fun game!

## WHAT YOU NEED

- 6 small items with strong scents, such as powdered spices, herbs or tumble dryer sheets
- 12 identical note cards
- art supplies, such as marker pens
- glue stick

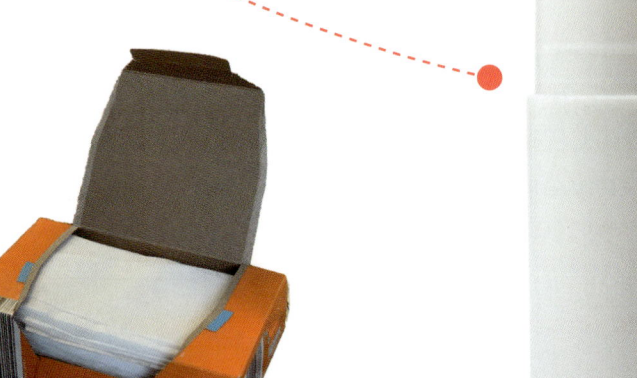

## WHAT YOU DO

### STEP 1
Collect six different scented items. They should be small and flat enough to fit on the backs of note cards. Items could include powdered spices, herbs or tumble dryer sheets.

### STEP 2
Decorate one side of each card. Swipe the glue stick on the undecorated sides of two cards. Take your first scented item and sprinkle or place it on the glue.

Repeat **step 2** to attach each scent to two cards.

### STEP 3
To play the game, mix up the cards and arrange them scent-side down on a table. Close your eyes. Then flip two cards and sniff them. If the cards are a match, leave them face up. If not, put them back. Continue until you've matched all six scents!

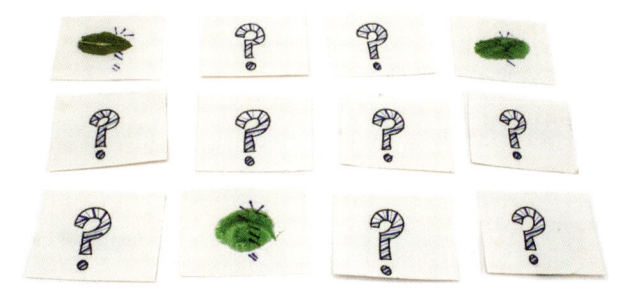

## WHAT YOU GET

**Nose neurons.** Your nose is home to millions of sensory neurons. Each neuron has a protein called an olfactory receptor. The receptors detect odour molecules. Neurons then send information about the odours to your brain. This allows you to experience the smell! **That's science!**

# DIY TEA SOAP

Turn tea leaves into a soap that cleans and **smells beau-tea-ful!**

## WHAT YOU NEED

- bar of soap
- cheese grater
- bowl
- tea bag
- cup of hot water
- scissors
- fork
- spoon
- silicon ice cube trays

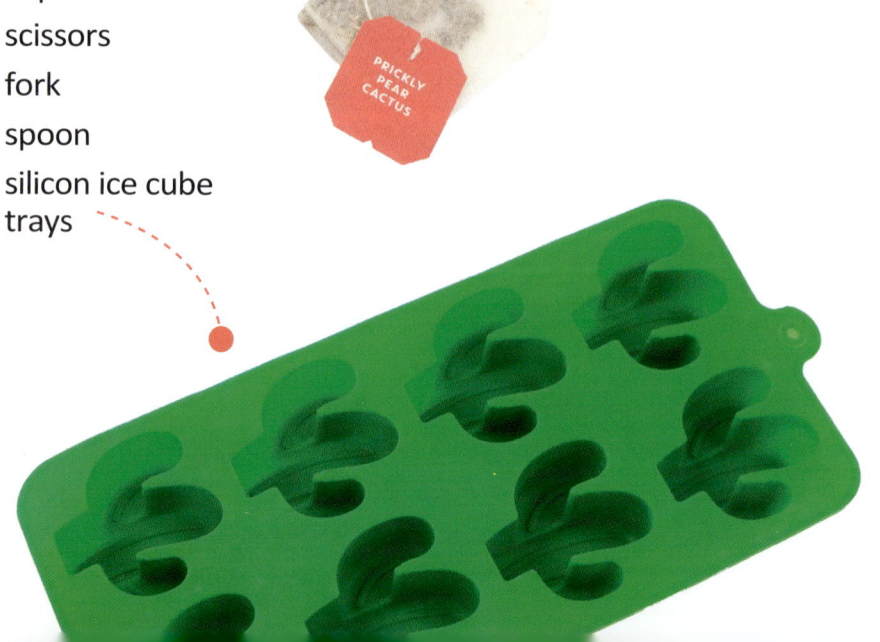

14

## WHAT YOU DO

### STEP 1
Use the cheese grater to grate the soap into a bowl.

### STEP 2
Dip the tea bag in a cup of hot water for several minutes.

### STEP 3
Pour the water into the bowl of soap. Cut open the tea bag and pour the leaves into the bowl. Let the bowl sit for about 30 minutes so the water soaks into the soap flakes.

### STEP 4
Mash the mixture together with a fork. Spoon it into ice cube trays and press down with the back of the spoon. Let the trays sit overnight.

### STEP 5
Pop the soaps out of the trays. Use one to wash your hands!

## WHAT YOU GET

**Amazing molecules.** Soap molecules have two ends. The head is attracted to water. The tail is attracted to oils and fats. In dirty water, soap molecules form clusters called micelles. The heads point outwards. The tails point inwards, trapping dirt and grease inside the micelle. The micelles wash away when rinsed with water. **That's science!**

# BIRTHDAY BATTER SLIME

Mix up a **sweet-smelling slime** worthy of a celebration!

SMELL-O-METER: 4

## WHAT YOU NEED

- hole punch
- cardstock in various colours
- medium mixing bowl & spoon
- 120 ml (½ cup) white PVA glue
- 120 ml (½ cup) water
- 2.5 ml (½ tsp) vanilla extract
- 180 ml (¾ cup) liquid starch

**EXPERIMENT!** WHAT OTHER SCENTS COULD YOU ADD TO SLIME? HOW DO THEY AFFECT THE SLIME'S LOOK AND FEEL?

16

## WHAT YOU DO

### STEP 1
Use the hole punch to cut confetti out of the cardstock.

### STEP 2
In a medium mixing bowl, mix together the glue and water.

### STEP 3
Add the vanilla and confetti. Mix well.

### STEP 4
Add 120 ml (½ cup) liquid starch. Knead the mixture until the slime is smooth and no longer sticks to your hands. If your slime stays sticky, add up to 60 ml (¼ cup) more starch. Close your eyes and smell the slime!

## WHAT YOU GET

**Slimy, smelly molecules.** Glue is made of long chains of molecules. The molecules flow past each other. Liquid starch causes the glue molecules to link together. This makes the glue thick and rubbery! Adding vanilla infuses the slime with odour molecules. **That's science!**

# SCENT SCRAPBOOK

Discover the powerful connection between scent and memory by creating an **odour-iffic scrapbook!**

## WHAT YOU NEED

- scented objects, such as pine needles, fresh cut grass or scented lotion
- paper
- scissors
- hole punch
- art supplies, such as marker pens, crayons, coloured pencils & glue
- split pins

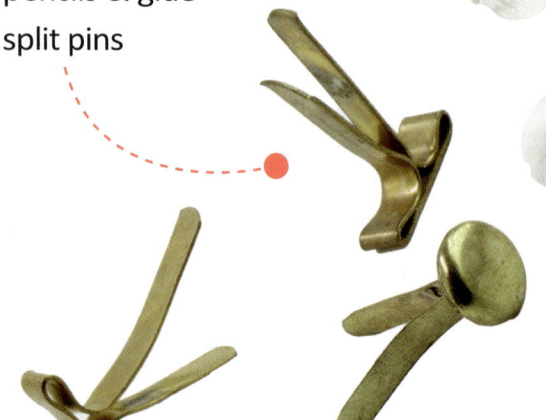

## WHAT YOU DO

### STEP 1
Collect scented items that remind you of specific memories, places or events. Items could include pine needles, freshly cut grass or scented lotion.

### STEP 2
Cut several sheets of paper in half. Stack the papers. Punch a hole in the top left corner of the stack. This is your scrapbook. Make a cover.

### STEP 3
On each inside page, draw a picture of the memory represented by each scent. Use glue to add the scented item into the image.

### STEP 4
Push a split pin through the hole to secure the pages together. Look through the scrapbook without smelling. Repeat, but this time inhale deeply as you look at each page. What do you notice?

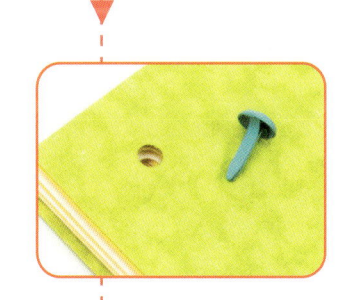

## WHAT YOU GET

**Brain power.** Scent has a stronger link to memory than any other sense. Scents are processed in your brain's olfactory bulb. This is directly connected to the parts of your brain that process emotions and memory. **That's science!**

# CALMING CRAYON CANDLE

Turn old art supplies into a relaxing candle that gives off a **calming scent** as it burns.

**EXPERIMENT! TRY ADDING DIFFERENT TYPES OF ESSENTIAL OILS TO DIFFERENT LAYERS.**

## WHAT YOU NEED

- candle wick
- scissors
- 50–100 old crayons
- craft knife
- glass bowl that can sit on top of a saucepan
- tin foil
- saucepan
- water
- whisk
- essential oil in a calming scent
- glass jar
- lighter, matches or candle warmer

## WHAT YOU DO

### STEP 1
Cut the wick about 6 cm longer than the jar is deep. Use a craft knife to slice vertically down a crayon wrapper. Peel the wrapper off. Repeat for each crayon.

### STEP 2
Line a glass bowl with tin foil. Break similarly coloured crayons into pieces and place in the bowl.

### STEP 3
Pour water into a saucepan so it is about 8 cm deep, and bring to a simmer. Put the glass bowl on top of the pan. Allow the crayons to melt.

### STEP 4
Remove the pan from heat. Whisk a few drops of essential oil into the bowl.

### STEP 5
Pour the melted wax into the jar. Put one end of the wick into the jar. Hold the top while the wax cools.

Repeat **steps 2 to 5** to add additional layers.

### STEP 6
Light your candle. What happens?

## WHAT YOU GET

**Smell release.** As the candle burns, the wax melts. The essential oil in the heated wax turns into gas. When a substance turns into gas, it releases more odour molecules. So, the burning candle has a strong smell. **That's science!**

# SEASON IN A JAR

What does spring smell like to you? **Capture the scents of each season** in a jar you can sniff anytime!

## WHAT YOU NEED

- scented items, such as cinnamon sticks, flower petals & leaves
- 4 jars with lids
- art supplies (optional)

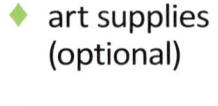

**EXPERIMENT!** ASK ANOTHER PERSON TO CLOSE THEIR EYES AND SMELL YOUR SEASON JARS. CAN THEY GUESS THE SEASON?

## WHAT YOU DO

### STEP 1
Collect items that remind you of each season, such as orange peels for winter or flower petals for spring.

### STEP 2
Place each season's items in a separate jar.

### STEP 3
Put the lids on the jars. Decorate each jar if you'd like.

### STEP 4
Close your eyes. Open each jar one at a time and breathe in the scent. What do you experience?

## WHAT YOU GET

**So many scents!** A human nose has more than 400 types of olfactory receptors. These allow us to detect more than 1 trillion different scents. Many seasonal scents bring up memories of holidays and other experiences. **That's science!**

# NOT-SO-STINKY SOCK

Aromatherapy means using natural, strongly scented oils to improve wellbeing. Explore **aromatherapy** as you turn an old sock into a sweet-smelling pal.

## WHAT YOU NEED

- 0.7–1 litre (3–4 cups) rice
- bowl
- essential oil
- spoon
- funnel
- sock
- twine
- art supplies that can safely be microwaved, such as felt & fabric glue
- microwave

**EXPERIMENT! TRY THIS PROJECT USING OTHER SCENTS. DO YOU NOTICE A DIFFERENCE IN HOW YOU FEEL?**

## WHAT YOU DO

### STEP 1
Pour the rice into a bowl. Add a few drops of essential oil and stir until the rice is coated.

### STEP 2
Use a funnel to pour the rice into the sock.

### STEP 3
Shake the sock so the rice settles to the bottom. Pinch the sock a few centimetres above the rice. Tie with a piece of twine to secure. Decorate your sock!

### STEP 4
Microwave your sock buddy in 30-second bursts until it is warm but not hot. Note how you feel. Now hold the sock close and breathe in the scent. Did your feelings change?

## WHAT YOU GET

**A mood changer.** Certain odours are thought to help you feel better. When inhaled, the smells cause a certain response in the brain. Lavender helps some people feel calm. A lemon scent may be able to improve your mood. **That's science!**

# SCRATCH & SNIFF PAINT

Mix up some scented paints to create a picture that **smells as good** as it looks!

## WHAT YOU NEED

- white PVA glue
- paint palette or egg carton
- food colouring
- craft sticks
- liquid scents, such as essential oils, almond extract & lemon juice
- paintbrush & paper

# WHAT YOU DO

### STEP 1
Squeeze the glue into each palette cup. If you don't have a palette, use an egg carton.

### STEP 2
Add a few drops of food colouring to each palette cup. Use craft sticks to stir in the food colouring.

### STEP 3
Add a few drops of scent to each colour. Use different scents for each one. Stir in the scents with craft sticks.

### STEP 4
Paint a picture and let it dry. Scratch each colour with your fingernail. What happens?

# WHAT YOU GET

**A scent masterpiece!** When you scratch the dried paint, the paint releases odour molecules into the air. The molecules are detected by the neurons in your nose. They send information about the scent to your brain. **That's science!**

# SMELLY TRAINER SWAB

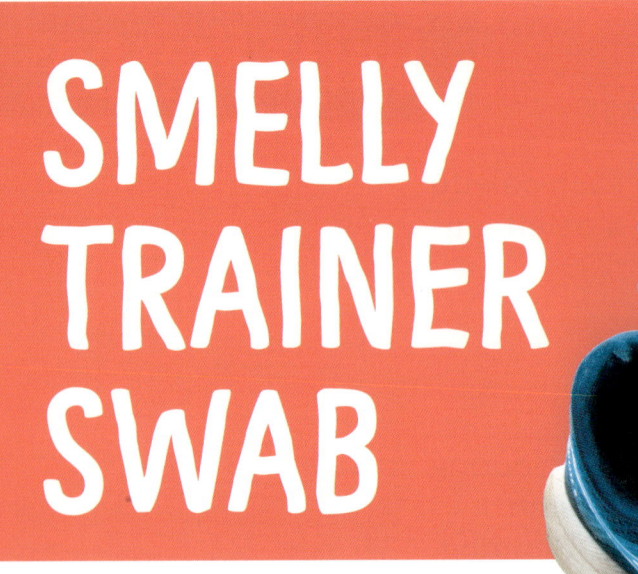

Does stinky really mean dirty? Find out by using your **smelliest trainers** to grow a bacteria garden.

## WHAT YOU NEED

- old, smelly trainers
- clean trainers
- 2 cotton swabs
- 2 petri dishes with agar
- tape
- marker pen

**EXPERIMENT! REPEAT THIS PROJECT WITH OTHER STINKY ITEMS, SUCH AS THE INSIDE OF A RUBBISH BIN.**

## WHAT YOU DO

### STEP 1
Swab the inside of a smelly trainer with a clean cotton swab.

### STEP 2
Lightly rub the swab back and forth in a zig-zag motion along the agar in a petri dish.

Repeat **steps 1 and 2** with the clean trainers.

### STEP 3
Use tape and a marker to label each petri dish with the type of trainer. Allow the petri dishes to sit in a warm place.

**2 WEEKS**

### STEP 4
Check on your petri dishes each day for 2 weeks. What do you notice? Which petri dish grows more bacteria?

## WHAT YOU GET

**Bacteria at work.** A human foot contains 125,000 sweat glands. The mix of sweat and the warm, damp environment of the shoe makes a perfect place for bacteria to grow. When the bacteria break down the sweat, they release a strong and stinky odour. **That's science!**

# FLOWER POWER

Find out which flowers attract which pollinators and **what scent has to do with it!**

## WHAT YOU NEED

- 2 flowers of the same colour, 1 with a strong scent and 1 with little to no scent
- 2 vases or jars of water
- notebook
- pencil

**EXPERIMENT!**
TRY PUTTING OTHER SCENTS, SUCH AS VANILLA OR LEMON, ON COTTON WOOL BALLS AND LEAVING THEM OUTSIDE. WHAT HAPPENS?

# WHAT YOU DO

### STEP 1
Collect two flowers of the same colour, one scented and one unscented, such as a white daisy and a gardenia.

### STEP 2
Place each flower in a vase or jar of water.

### STEP 3
Put the flowers outside in a warm, sunny green space. The flowers should be about 3 metres (10 feet) apart from each other.

### STEP 4
Observe your flowers every 10 to 15 minutes for several hours. Take notes on which pollinators, such as bees, wasps and butterflies, visit which flowers. Does one flower get more visitors than the other?

## WHAT YOU GET

**Pollinator preference.** Most plants use their scent to attract pollinators. Flies and bees prefer sweet scents. Beetles prefer musty, fruity or spicy scents. A plant's scent is strongest when it is ready for pollination. **That's science!**

# FIND OUT MORE

## BOOKS

*10-Minute Crafty Projects* (10-Minute Makers), Elsie Olson (Raintree, 2022)

*I Can Be a Science Detective: Fun STEM Activities for Kids*, Claudia Martin (Dover Publications, 2019)

*You Smell!: And So Does Everything Else*, Clive Gifford (Laurence King Publishing, 2019)

## WEBSITES

**dkfindout.com/uk/human-body/senses/nose-and-smell**
Discover more about the senses with DKFindout!

**wonderlabplus.sciencemuseumgroup.org.uk/make-and-do**
The Science Museum has lots of science projects on their website for you to try.

**www.bbc.co.uk/bitesize/topics/zgdmsbk**
BBC Bitesize has lots of information about the senses.